the Book of Olympio

Life is like being on top of an empty building. Although the center is the safest place to be, if you can live on the edge without falling, you would be able to see what is both on top, as well as what is at the bottom. Only then you can truly get a sense of what is all around you. Only then can you fully sense life.

Humans value others based on
their looks, possessions, abilities
and even their ancestors' history.
This is our nature. Therefore, a rat
will still be a rat even if it no
longer carries disease.
A Frenchman will still be French,
even if spotted in a shithole,
and until history tells us
otherwise, a Black man will be
Black.

What you regularly put in your stomach will end up showing on your skin.

Racism is part of our nature, negative but natural. It is a disease created by ignorance from which everyone suffers, some of us are just sicker than others. The only cure is forgiveness. Through this, we create room for each other, and only then we can work together on our differences. That racist is not your monster, just another family.

No, I don't sketch out my visions,
I just make them happen.

Having "style" doesn't matter
whether you are wearing a paper
bag or an army shields.
Or whether you sing opera or
jazz. You still smell the same.

To get out of the house, you have to be able to think outside of the house.

Never regret missing an exit, you never know what is on the other side of the highway.

The only way to tell the truth is
to say it exactly the way it feels,
any other way would be a lie.

It is all about how far you can see.

I have crossed the limit of
pleasure, it felt like death.
Death wasn't as intriguing as I
thought it would be.
It was just a continuation of life.

I wear my clothes till they
become mine, that is when I like
them the most.

I am not always satisfied with my work, but when they are done, I let them go. Perhaps they control me more than I thought.

Unless you have truly
experienced something, you
know nothing about it.

At the end of the day, we all just want a color we can relate to.

When you know what you know because of what you know, you can only live with confidence.

I am not much interested in
creativity but self-expression.
The difference being what comes
from the heart as opposed from
the head.

Every now and then, it comes
across as a game of golf.
A shot that cannot be taken
unless you see it. Yes, we are
talking about painting.

Blue is deep, sexy, dangerous, powerful, frightening, limitless, beautiful. Like the sky and the ocean. Love is blue.

When you keep your eyes on something for so long, you end up losing it. It gets blurry.

The only respect you will ever get is that which you earn, respect does not come with luck.

There is no road longer than the one that gets you closer to yourself.

Art is not in the eye of the
beholder, beauty is.
Art is art.
Art is self expression, nothing
more, nothing less.

The only person with the ability
to truly see you is yourself.
To the rest of the world, you will
only be as you were last seen.

Addiction is natural yet misunderstood. It freaks people out when they learn that you are addicted to something. Even if that something is as simple as water, food, sex or sleep. Addiction is the only disease that even the victim is forced to say the name of and is considered less as a disease and more as a crime.

There is a place that cannot be
felt without being numb.
A disease that cannot be cured
without being sick.
Knowledge that cannot be
reached without losing your
mind. A life that cannot be lived
without dying.

Love comes from happiness. Happiness comes from satisfaction. Satisfaction comes from good health, working towards your dreams and becoming yourself.

The deeper your artistic spirit becomes, the harder it is to see the difference between beautiful and ugly.

We are afraid of things that are larger than ourselves or that greatly differ from who we think we are. At times, people who are similar to us become a threat because we don't trust ourselves enough to have others like us around so we spent our lives running. Running away from everything including ourselves. Running away to feel safe.

We are becoming lonely creatures but too weak to look each other in the eyes and take a chance. We use our power to create things that are supposed to connect us but which only divide. We are the most lost creatures on the planet, and it is only going to get worse. No one to blame. We are only becoming who we are.

I have found myself in the most
disgraceful situations a human
being can experience.
Yet, I would not trade those
experiences for a million dollars.
It changed everything.
It is like having a baby for the
first time.

Quotes are like a splash of paint
on a blank canvas.
They can't always be explained.
They are like poetry.

Rule #1: Never argue with someone who is just following orders. You will lose your ribs

I have drowned so deeply for so long that I forget how much the people around me have to do to catch up.

Being yourself is more complicated than it should be. We are trained to see and what to be. Deprived of our true nature because stupid people rule the world and who have the passion to do so. Expressing yourself is the only way to become yourself, and only then can you see your true nature, create a connection, fall in love, be satisfied and happy. Being satisfied with who you are is very important. Satisfaction creates happiness, and happiness is the answer. Without happiness, love does not grow.

Loving is giving.
Loving is sharing positive energy.
The way we feel affects the way
we see and treat others.
You cannot give something you
don't have.
You cannot give love if you don't
feel love.

So, if you care about others, you want to create a better future. Stop talking about it or hiding behind those stupid peace and love signs. Start working on your own happiness. A happy person is like a big tree touched by a fresh breeze in a park. He doesn't need to do anything but just stick around. A happy person is love.

Think about your own happiness without getting in the way of others. Help people if you can but know that your own happiness is what's first needed.

Who you are lies somewhere in
between who you truly are, and
who you are not.

When you feel healthy, nothing feels impossible.

Love is a beautiful, strong and resilient flower that can survive anywhere. But remember, money is water.

Life is a form of art.
As is painting, music and sex.
Money is the art materials.

What you do does not make who you are. What you cannot do without does.

Whatever inspires you to get up in the morning can also make you fall. And what you cannot live without can kill you.

When you wake up every day, work hard and do the right thing, you start developing a level of respect for yourself. A respect strong enough to show on your skin, which the world has no choice but to respect.

I have nothing but shitty advice that would either set you free or bury you alive with pride. Don't waste your time with me, I'm not a gray guy.

When you do something that is not in your true nature, no matter how good or successful you are at it, it will kill you.

Once you realize how easy it is
to get dirt under your fingernails,
you will never look down on
another human being again.

I don't stop when it looks good.
I only stop when I feel
completely trapped with no exit.
I am a flying slave.

We are not good enough to know
how good other animals are.

7 things to experience to better understand yourself and the rest of the world:

Travel
Parenting
Poverty
Wealth
Living your passion
Insanity
Addiction

The truth lies in between the two extremes.

A true winner is the one who knows how to let go.

Love is a seed that cannot grow without space. To love someone is to automatically and subconsciously give them space for their seed to grow. Loving is giving, you cannot give something you don't have. You cannot love without that space.

Life is pretty simple, you just need to be able to watch the paint dry.

When who you truly are is bigger than you are, you have no choice but to go with the ride.

It takes intelligence to find happiness.

Once you understand, you know what to do.

Running like dancing.
Have a good playlist, let the music take over and feel the movement of every muscle in your body. Let the songs lead you. Never worry about losing control or making unfamiliar moves. Live like you run.

Life is a drug. The higher you get, the harder you crash.

Sometimes the difference is
nothing more than the distance.

Drugs make you weak mentally and physically. Once you are weak, you lose your confidence. Once you lose your confidence, you lose yourself. After losing yourself, you lose everything. Drugs are your enemies friends.

A world of confidence.
A world so confident no one has to be anything but themself. No need to be afraid of facing the truth. No need to create heaven. No need to be ashamed at being called fat – it is not an insult, just a description. A world so confident, age is just a number and wrinkles bring a different type of beauty to look forward to. Being called beautiful is not a compliment – it is just a trait with which you were born. Like the money you inherited from your grandfather. A world so confident intelligence is nothing more than luck and hating me is nothing personal. It's only human nature and together we can laugh about.
No class of any kind because we are all equals and only the lowest classes would try to get in the way of others' happiness.
Imagine a world of confidence.

We are what satisfies us.

A work of Art has nothing to do with beauty, ugliness or creativity. There is nothing a work of Art needs to do or be but Art. Art is self-expression, nothing more, nothing less. If there is anything something needs to do or be, then that thing is not Art. We are all artists in a way, some expressions are just more valued than others in this society for different reasons, some good and some stupid. I personally think animals are the greatest artist on the planet. And you don't need to be involved with any form of art to be an artist. Art is not what you do, but what you are.

Anyone you can imagine has some kind of dignity for themselves. A dignity that can never be taken away.

No one chooses to fall.

You make a better future by keeping yourself healthy each day for the next.

The only thing stronger than love
is passion.

The art world has nothing to do with art.

There is a fine line between a genius and an idiot.

If you are going to run faster than your eyes, you might as well run with out them.

An artist can see the future.

Guns don't protect anyone. They only result in a quicker death. Is that hard to see?

If the finish line doesn't stop you,
nothing will.

I don't think much about where I
came from and I'm glad I don't.
It would only be a reminder of
how far I have come and create a
comfort I'm not ready for.
I have come a long way.

I can hear voices of the colors in my head.

I can hear voices of the colors in my head.

Art is not a movement but personal. Do your own thing

There is a difference between
living and choosing a life.

The system is set up to keep you down when you fall.

The most fascinating thing I
found with humans is the ability
to end up accepting reality,
whatever that ends up being.

If you know where I go every
time I die a little, you would beg
to die with me a little.

Respect what you have. It is all you have.

You can't be inspired if you are not in touch with yourself.

True self-expression is like freestyle dancing, you cannot plan every step or you will stumble.

We all have something in common; our nature, human nature. We have the ability to work together and even get along, but that will never happen unless we stop pretending to be something we are not.

First, you have to show up.

By the time I'm done, my piece
leaves me no space for signature.
I have come close to myself.

I don't need my brain in order to continue painting, it's my heart I'm concerned about.

Sometimes people are not good enough to know how good other people are.

In painting, colors are ways of communication and travel, like instruments and music. You can never have enough if played right.

It's ok, just remember to be neat
in your mess.

In order to find yourself, you have to break yourself.

I am who I am because of
who I am.

When you live in a small space,
you can only paint small.

Forgive me, I've lost a quote.

It is never about what you do but the way you do it.

The only way to discover your true self is to completely let go of the mind and follow only the heart.

Reality can never completely feel real. Part of us will always be a dream.

ISBN: 978-0-5783281-6-4

Kodjovi Olympio

CPSIA information can be obtained
at www.ICGtesting.com
Printed in the USA
LVHW102338200322
713959LV00004B/455